Fortune Cookies

Volume 3

Dr. Kareem Pottinger

YSD Publishing House

Library of Congress Catalog in
Publication Data

YSD PUBLISHING HOUSE
14490 Coastal Bay Circle 13204
Naples, FL. 34119

Library of Congress Catalog Card
Number:
2013934185
International Standard Book
Number 978-1-937171-02-5

Dedicated to my firstborn

YOUNGSABATH POTTINGER

If I ever leave this planet, I have
always kept you in mind.

Not leavening my wisdom far behind

Grow Good

INTRODUCTION

The true intent of this book
was to write a set of guidelines
that could be
immediately implemented in
the progress and advancement
of my sons elite
life.
This vast deep knowledge was
to be used as a
tool
to keep him far beyond just,
"ahead of the learning curb" for
lack of better expression.
These
rules are the widely accepted
and used unspoken
secrets amongst the elite in
which we use to rear our

young.
Although these are our
secrets
and most of us will and should
be extremely displeased for
having them on display for the
"normal's" of the world to
receive, I decided to release
them nevertheless.
For,
upon reading the finished
piece I realized that these elite
secrets
could not only serve to benefit
my son and family to come
well, but that the entire
world
could serve to benefit from
these lists of guidelines.
The way that this book is
intended to be received is to

ponder upon each page for a complete 24 hours.
Each page is to be pondered upon for the whole day; it is to be used as topic of discussion for that day amongst peers, friends, and family members' etcetera.
It is especially designed to be pondered upon mostly by you. For a complete 24 hours deep thought on each subject should be pondered upon. The reason being is to see how these guidelines could be implemented into your current life, how should they have been implemented in your past life, and how can they benefit your future.

It
is only through the true
belief
and usage of these
guidelines
that your life's
works will be greatly
affected
in its progress.

Live
for
yourself,
if not then you
run the
risk
of
becoming
a
very
unhappy
elderly

You have to make the time to catch-up with yourself in life, in order for you to understand the true value of the position that you hold in life

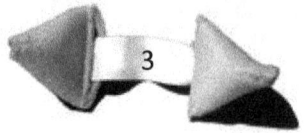

*Becoming
an
adult
is
about
having
a
true
conviction
of
yourself*

*You
only
get
one-shot
at
life
so
make
this
one
worthwhile*

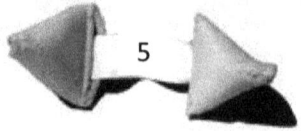

*Life
passes
by
you
fast,
especially
when
you
do not
value
every
moment*

*When trying to
succeed;
planning
is the key,
you have to
plan
everything
while being
aware of the
tiniest
of
details*

*The
bad
that
you
do
in
life,
will
always
outweigh
the
good*

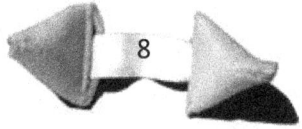

You should always be trying to do better in life; for the moment that you think you have reached perfection, is the very moment that you stop aspiring to the top

Just because the concept the concept did not change, does not mean that it has not evolved

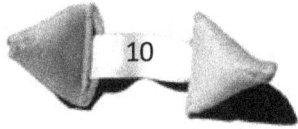

*It is very
important
not to break
the bonds that
you make in
this life
because
they are the
only things that
are holding you
up in this
world*

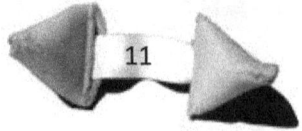

*Your
mind
is your
one
true-friend
and
it is the
one-friend
that you should
pay the closest
attention
to*

*Always
keep
in
mind
that your
efforts
will
become
meaningless
without
any
results*

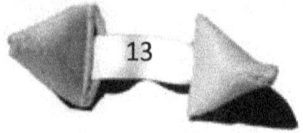

No operation
goes directly as
planned;
when it doesn't
you don't go
berserk
but
in turn
you calm down
and tie-up
the
loose-ends

*The
only
person
that
can
get
you
into
problems
is
yourself*

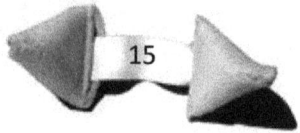

*Sometimes your
good
isn't good
enough
and you must
fail
in order
to actually
learn
how to
become
good enough*

*Certain
people's
mentality
are
just
like
wild-elephants,
they
cannot
be
reasoned
with*

Deceptions
sole purpose
is to hide;
so upon being
deceived,
it is more
important to
seek what that
deception was
trying to hide
as oppose to
why

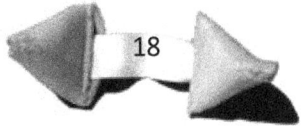

*When a person
that has
something
to say
says
nothing,
their
silence
can be so
loud
that it becomes
deafening*

*Life is a
constant
cycle
of
sun-ups
and
sun-downs;
the sooner you
realize this the
more
poised
you will become*

*Following
through
with your
conceptions
will be
the only
way
for you
to
actualize
those
conceptions*

*Work
smart
and
opportunities
will
follow*

*If the people
that you have
chosen
to be around
cannot help you
evolve
and
grow,
then you need
to pick new
people to be
around*

*It
will
always
be
time
for
you
to
take
the
initiative*

*Trouble cost
money,
money cost
time,
and
time
is
something
that
you
cannot
get back*

*Having
problems
and then
solving them,
teaches
you the type of
responsibility
that you need
to acquire
in order to
maintain your
goals*

One of the
happiest
moments
in a parent's
life
is to see their
children
succeed and to
succeed
in a
great-way
is
tops

*Be careful;
everyone's
secretly
got their
pad
out going
for the
same
things
that
your
are*

You
can't
win
a
heart
that
already
has
someone
else
in
it

*It is very
important to
remember that
after each
dark
storm-cloud in
your life,
the sun will
come out
to
shine
once-again*

*Even though
the
light
is
green,
it
doesn't
mean
that the
coast
is
clear*

*Your life
style
has to be
in
congruence
with where
you want to
end-up
or
you will
not
end-up there*

*You should
always keep in
mind that we
as human
beings always
do
what it occurs
for us
to do
at
the
time*

*Sometimes you
have to learn
to become
more-selfish
for
yourself
or
there will be
no
accomplishing
what you need
to get done*

*In order to
accomplish the
dreams that
you have
in life,
you are going to
have to create
a
starting-point
towards
your
visions*

You must have
safeguards
in
life
and it is very
important
to
know
that
those
safeguards
work

In
life
you
should
always
be
focused
on
accelerating
your
end-game

*Always keep in
mind that the
people
in this
world
will always act
and look
like, what they
believe
about
themselves to
be true*

In
order
to
secure
your
future
you
must
lay-down
a
foundation

*Don't ever get
too
comfortable to
where
you
do not
want
to
step-up
to
the
next-level*

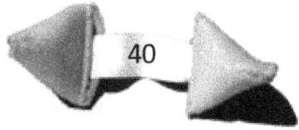

*It is important
to understand
the fact that
throughout your
life the people
that will appear
in it, will come
and go;
everyone
is on
there on
path*

*The
shortest
path
to
victory
is
to
build
a
winning
team*

*Good
connections
will
never
hurt
a
business*

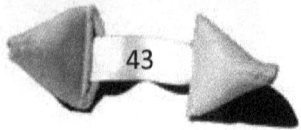

The
correct
decisions
will
not
be
made
when
fueled
by
franticness

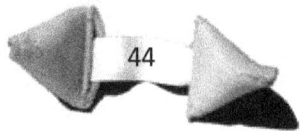

*When you
believe
in yourself,
it makes it a lot
easier for
other
people
to
believe
in
you
as well*

When a person possesses quiet-confidence, they feel that they don't have to speak because they know what they are capable off

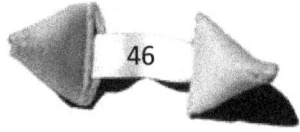

*The
last
of
the
leeches
are
the
hardest
ones
to
get
rid-of*

*Learning
how to
put
things
behind
you
and
move-on
is key
to a happy
and
successful life*

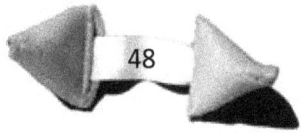

*Sometimes
a
parent
can
tell
when
a
child's
mistake
is
on its
way*

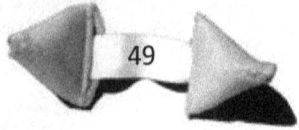

*If you
do not do
business
the way its
being
offered,
then
opt
not
to do
the
business*

*In life in order
to succeed you
must maximize
your abilities
and you cannot
do so without
first learning
what the
limit
is of the
things that
you can do*

When a
person
does not have
to
work, then
they're going
to be
lazy
on the
job
that you give
them

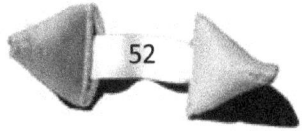

Your dreams, your goals, your aspirations, your predetermined achievements, is your new home; it is where you need to live in order to accomplish them

*No-one
will
ever
take
care
of
your
things
the
way
that
you will*

*If
you
are
afraid
of
the
answer,
do
not
ask
the
question*

*A
good
plan
should
and
always
will
be
flexible*

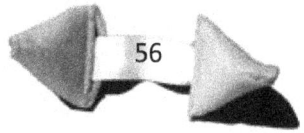

*You have to
think of
your mind
much like an
animal
that must be
trained
in the
way
that you want
it to
act*

*Do
not
allow
yourself
to
fade,
and
you
wont*

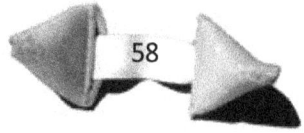

*It's important
to
understand
that whatever
the
dominating
thoughts are
in your mind,
that is who you
will become
and how you
will act*

*Hate
your
opponent
and
you
will
never
give
less
than
100
percent*

*It
is
never
smart
to
work
stupid*

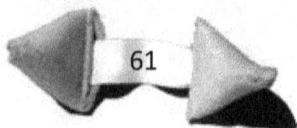

*Being
patient
allots
for
less
mistakes*

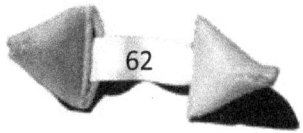

*Happiness
will
always
belong
to
the
ones
that
follows
their
vision*

Procure
the
necessaries

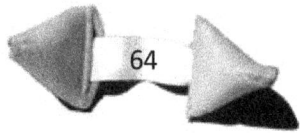

*Things happen
in
life
that you cannot
undo
and the
things
that you
cannot
undo should
not be
dwelled upon*

*Sometimes
one
mistake
is
one
too
many*

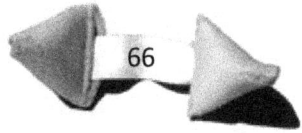

The
best
way
to
chase
something
is
to
let
it
chase
you

Things just don't happen without a reason, there is always a reason for the things that are happening or have happened

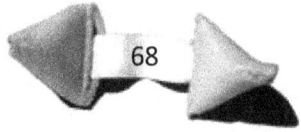

You
do
not
always
get
a
choice
in
life
to do
things
differently

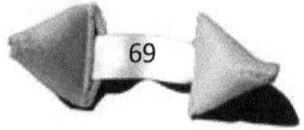

The
tighter
your
plan
the more
likely
you
will
run
into
something
unpredictable

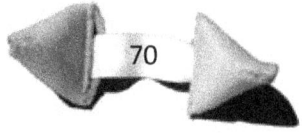

*You
have
to
push
your
limit
in
order
to
progress*

Upon making decisions; always take everything and everything meaning all-things into consideration

You
have
to
lose
sometimes
in
order
to
learn
how
to
win

You
shouldn't
take the
cake
out
of
the
oven
until
it is
completely
baked

Things come easier when your being smarter

*You
receive
exactly
what
you
send
out
in
life*

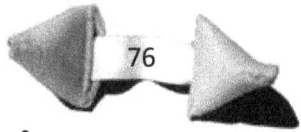

*Don't
forget
who
you originally
were
as you
rise
to the
top and you
will always
stay
grounded*

*You
have to
go
with the
top
people
in order
to
keep
your
dreams
alive*

*Go
with
your
gut
most
times,
it
will
never
lead
you
wrong*

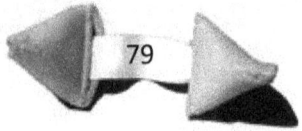

*In
life
you
only
get
what
you
are
prepared
to
struggle
for*

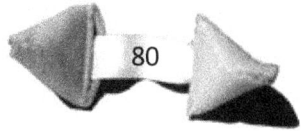

*Fast
money
always
fades
fast*

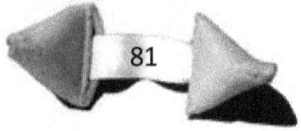

No matter how long you have been acquainted, it is difficult to truly know a person

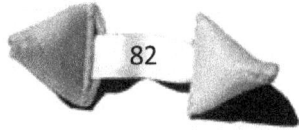

*Things
on the
surface
are
never
really
what
they
seem,
there is always
an
under-tow*

*People
have a
need
for
leadership
and
if
you are willing
to take that
role,
they
will follow*

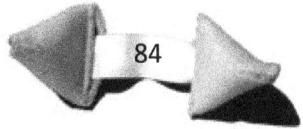

*It
is
your
job
to
bring
your
vision
to
life*

When
you
are
winning
is
when
you
should
press
even
harder

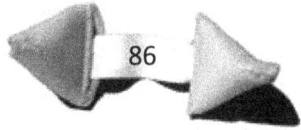

*When it comes
time
to
accomplishing
one
of
your goals,
you must push
everything
as far
as you
can*

*Your
life
should
be
about
how you
feel
and
how you
want
to
feel*

It
is
your
job
to
make
the
impossibilities
in your life,
work
for
you

*The more
that you know
about the
person
you would like
to become,
the easier
it will be
to
become
that
person*

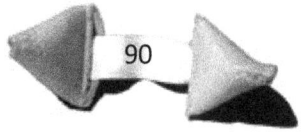

*You
shouldn't
argue
with
good-results
when
things
don't
go
exactly
as
planned*

*Sometimes
the
things
that
you
can't
see
are
coming
up
next*

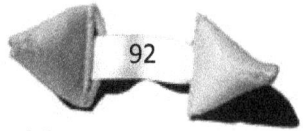

*Small
things
can
and
will
hold-up
big
things*

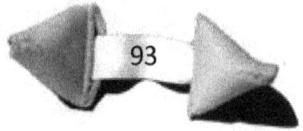

*The
decisions
that
we are
consistently
making
is
what is
continuously
shaping
our
lives*

*That
was then
and
this is
now;
always
seems to
present
a
difference
in
ability*

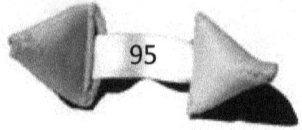

*The
conclusions
to
your
life
is
in
your
hands*

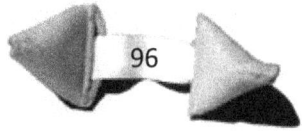

*Some will
see
random-news,
while
others
will see
opportunity
for the
same-exact
situation;
which one are
you*

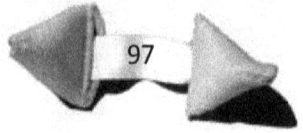

Intuitive improvisation is the secret of genius

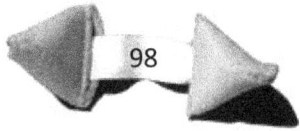

*Proper
prior
preparation
will
always
prevent
a
horrible
performance*

*The
world's
rarest
commodity
is
certainty
in
an
uncertain
world*

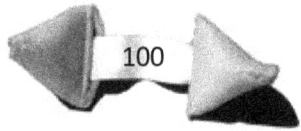

You should always start with what comes first

*It
is important
to know
what you
know
and
to know
of the things
that
you
do not
know*

*Always keep in
mind that
your
cold-stakes
can
heat-up
while
your
hot-stakes
are
cooling
down*

*The key to
victory
is
anticipation;
the
ability to
see the
future
and
react
to
it*

*You can
turn
an
occasional
negative
into a
plus
by learning
how to
manage
your
mistakes*

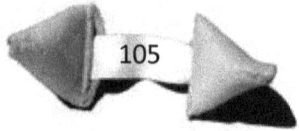

It's uncertain to
know
if the
good-times
will
last long
so
enjoy
and
take
full
advantage

*Sometimes
an
incredible
future
will
start
of
slow*

*Every
person you will
ever
encounter
will always
be
based
on
their
mind;
including
you*

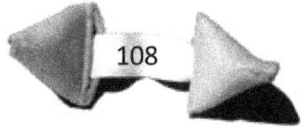

Quantity changes quality

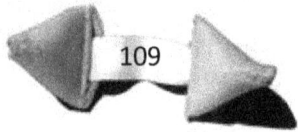

*On
vacation,
any
way
that
you
go
is
the
right-way*

When the time is right for an idea, nothing can stop it

*Destiny
is only a
destination
that
you set
for yourself by
the
actions
that
you are
performing
today*

You
are
never
to
consider
yourself
stupid
for
trying

*Persisting
and
being patient
is the
drive
that you
cannot lose
focus on
when
trying to
achieve your
goals*

When people show you who they are, please believe them

*Understand
the
fact that even
though
your
plan
may be
simple,
it
may not
come along
easy*

*Many times
you will
have to
fall
just so
that
you can
learn how to
stand-up
in that
particular
situation*

*Sometimes
you
will
never
know
what
you
need
until
you
need
it*

Do not
wait
for
risk
to be the
only move that
you have
left
in order
for you
to
take-one

*You can
only
win-big
depending
on
what
type of
game
you
decide
to
play*

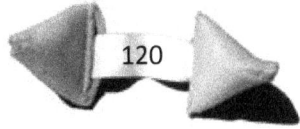

Always keep in mind that people may build you up just to tear you down

*In the
race
to the
top;
hundreds will
start
but
only
the
determined
will
finish*

*It's
silly
to
suffer
when
you
can
afford
not
too*

*In
life
a
person
turns
into
nothing,
without
integrity*

Depending
on how a
person
thinks
is
what
will
determine
how
that
person
lives

A person that is a shadow will be unable to exist without its master

*Water
the
flowers
that
you
want
to
survive*

*Making a great
deal of
positive
and
forward
momentum
towards
your
goal,
should always
be your
objective*

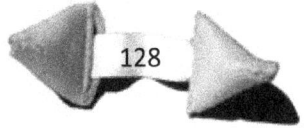

Beneath
every
glossy-surface
is
a
world
full
of
gliding-monster

*Your life
will
not
last
forever
so
start
doing
what
you
want
now*

*Any
compromises
leads
to a
lack
of
respect
for the
person
doing
the
compromising*

*Those
who
have
been
wounded
by
you;
only
want
one
thing,
revenge*

*Listen
to
your
thoughts
before
you
speak
them*

Imagine a
life
better than the
one you are
living
right now
and
do
something
about it
to get
there

*What
you
want
is
what
you
should
be
working
for*

*Everything
is
possible;
you
just
need
to
know
how
to
do
it*

*The art
of
great-business
is to never let
your emotions
or personal
feelings
interfere
with
your
decision
making*

*No
one
will
live
your
life
for
you*

*At some point
people
will
start
to
recognize
the
positive
of the
things
that you are
doing*

Don't
live
in
a
way
of
trying
to
deceive
yourself

Make sure that when you are practicing, you are practicing correctly because the way how you practice is the way how you are going to perform

*When you
have
lost your
heart
through
fear
the only way
to
win
it back, is to
conquer
that fear*

*Always
remember
that
some
of us
as
human-beings
are
more
broken
than
others*

*Do not
put
all
your
hopes
into
a
promise
that
was
never
made*

The
only
way
to
truly
know your
limits
is
to
exceed
pass
them

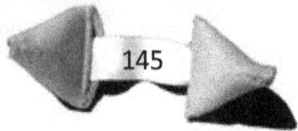

*You
can't
break
something
that
is
already
broken*

*It
is
best
to
always
look
around
and
consider
all
your
options*

You should always take the time to listen

What
is
your
baseline,
you cannot
acquire
a
fantastic
life
without
a
baseline

You
shouldn't
make
a
big
decision
on
a
notion

*Less time
talking,
more
time thinking,
and
even a greater
amount of time
doing,
should be your
golden rule in
achieving
anything*

*There
is
always
going
to be
an
underbelly,
just
wait
to
see
it*

You

should

not

make

big

decisions

until

you

know

what will

come

next

*Think about
what
you are
going
to do
because
once
done,
it
can not
be
undone*

*You
can't
really
hold
a
person
that
has
a
damaged
mind,
responsible*

*A person
will
always
only
be as
good
as
their
word,
so
pay
attention*

156

Be smart
when
it
is
your
time
because
you
do not
stay
hot
forever

*When
trying
to
succeed
in
a
great
way,
you
need
an
edge*

*In life
it
will
rarely
be
as
simple
as
what
it
appears
to be*

The End

Additional books written by
Dr. Kareem Pottinger available online at

and your local book stores nationwide

<u>FORTUNE COOKIES VOLUMES 1-11</u>

also   available   on   your

<u>Kindle</u>   <u>Nook</u>   <u>Apple</u>   <u>devices</u>